SMALL SOULS

Meditations for children

Roxanne Paynter

Published by:
Joshua Books
P.O. Box 5149, Maroochydore BC
Queensland Australia 4558

All correspondence to the publisher
at the above address.

© Copyright Roxanne Paynter
First Printed 2003
Reprinted 2004

Distributed by:
Joshua Books
1300 888 221

ISBN 0 9581891 0 2

Category: New Age: Self Help: Author

Joshua Books

Thoughts on "SMALL SOULS"

"As a Behaviour Support Teacher, we often incorporate calming strategies and visualisation within our work. Roxanne's meditations are perfect! Her work is very imaginative and vivid; within seconds of reading you have 'moved' into a very calm and safe environment. Fantastic meditations that would appeal to both children and adults alike."

- Kelly O'Grady
(B.Ed., M.Ed.)

"I thought this was beautifully written. It gave vivid images, which let your imagination take you to different places. I could actually smell and feel them. It helped me to relax and escape from day to day pressures, so I will use them myself also."

- Julie Medhurst (Mother)
Mt Gambier, South Australia

"I felt myself being drawn to these magical, mystical places that you've created with words. I have actually used your Rainbow and Waterfall to work through my own pain, and the feelings associated with chronic pain. I am certain that anyone who experiences these meditations will be left with peaceful and inspirational thoughts and feelings, just as I have."

- Kylie Nash (Nurse and Mother)
Arundel, Queensland

"These meditations calm the mind and soothe the soul. Just a few minutes reading achieves an amazing calming and uplifting feeling. They promote a feeling of wellbeing and also help you to cope with life's difficult situations."

- Sally Badcock (Mother)
Scottsdale, Tasmania

"A collection of wonderful meditations with insight into alleviating anxiety and fears. The power of words and relaxing travels take you to a quiet place of understanding within."

- Gayle Edwards (Mother)
Everton Hills, Queensland

"Teaching children the skill to visualise, or meditate, can be beneficial in reducing the stress levels children and young adults deal with in their daily interactions. Guided meditations such as Roxanne's are part of my repertoire and I have included some of hers to my collection. Her collection will appeal to boys as well as girls and across a range of ages."

- Lucia Nickolson
(Reiki Master, Advisory Teacher-Behaviour)

"There's a need for everyone to enjoy some peaceful moments. These meditations are just the thing and there's something there for everyone."

- Tina Hammant

"Congratulations Roxanne for this inspirational work of art. Through self expression of mind, body and soul we can create a living canvas. Colourful in freedom of thought, hopes and dreams, doubts and fears. A truly rewarding experience for both parent and child as it encourages a greater communication and understanding for one another."

- Michelle Holyhead (Mother)
Sunshine Coast, Queensland

ALSO BY ROXANNE PAYNTER

SOUL SAFARI

Meditations for Life

INDEX

Dedicated to my small souls,
Jordan & Lane.

Roxanne Paynter

Roxanne Paynter was born in Tasmania, Australia and lives in Queensland with her husband and two children.

Roxanne is an outstanding young woman who has risen above challenge in her own life to write this simple and practical book that will help our children to a better and richer life through meditation and creative visualization.

True heroes go about their routine business of living, laughing and loving with high hopes and good principles. They do all things to the best of their ability. They do not seek accolades or recognition but they do touch our hearts and make a difference in our lives.

A MESSAGE FROM THE AUTHOR

At age 28 my first child was born. My son spent the first few months of his life in intensive care. We did not know from one day to the next if he would survive.

During this time I had the opportunity to discover how difficult it is with a sick child of any age. I knew my son would be a little different, and I thought about how I could make him feel good about himself as he grew older. I analysed the things that would be most important to teach him.

Through research and reading I discovered these things to be love, self esteem, and a connection to spirit or purpose in life. I then searched for a tool that would help me pass these things on. I found nothing and saw a need for a book like "Small Souls".

I realised that meditation was the simplest, most effective way to do this for many reasons. Not only does the child benefit from relaxation, and stimulating their imagination, but they are empowered to draw on their own abilities. They learn that they are important, and that they have purpose.

For parents, these meditations are simple, effective and create a bonding experience with the child. They address every-day issues, and parents choose what is appropriate for their child.

Roxanne Paynter

INTRODUCTION

Most parents would agree that their children are more precious than anything else they've known. We monitor and nurture our children's physical wellbeing, but how do we go about developing a child's inner growth? Now, more than ever, our children need the ability to function and survive in a world where we cannot protect them from harsh realities.

Our children need to know that their lives have purpose, and that they are connected to others around them. It is from this sense of spirituality that comes morals. values and self esteem. Traditional religious practices seem inappropriate to some parents, yet they still wish to develop a sense of spirit in their child. 'Small Souls' aims to assist you develop your child's individual growth.

Not all children are destined to be great academics, but by recognising the importance of self esteem, we can at least provide the skills to cope with what life brings. Lack of self esteem can inhibit learning and creativity. By acknowledging a child's strong emotion and seeing their reality, they feel valued and respected. This helps create a unique soul that is able to draw upon their own resources.

Through meditations, we are able to empower children with words. In a relaxed and peaceful state, we can focus on specific issues. It may be that your child is un-happy or grieving, in which case we can focus on security or healing. Children can use their own creativity for problem solving. For children ill or confined, they may simply benefit from relaxation and using their imagination.

The effectiveness of these meditations lies ultimately with the reader. It is most important that the child is content to rest or lie down while you read. Bedtime is probably appropriate for most children. Encourage the child to close their eyes, and breathe slowly and deeply. Breathing in this manner helps the child to relax their body, and frees their mind to wander. Try to make your tone of voice calm and soothing. Feel free to add names or places that you know your child would enjoy or relate to.

By investing your energies in the development of your child's soul, you enrich their lives more than any other gift you could give. Not only giving them greater coping skills, you add magic to the mundane. You enable the child to connect spiritually when you are apart, helping your Small Soul to become a Great Soul.

Being at the beach
brings my senses alive.

SEASIDE

Standing on the sand, you are watching the ocean. Imagine that your breathing is the sound of waves gently crashing on the shore. You breathe slowly and deeply. The sun is warm on your body, and you feel happy and relaxed.

Looking down, you see the water lapping at your toes. Wriggle them in the sand. The soft breeze carries the smell of salty water to your nose. Inhale deeply, and let the invigorating air fill your lungs. Enjoy how the beach makes you feel. The cheery sunlight sparkles on the water as the waves roll and tumble. You are calm and peaceful.

Looking to the sky you see birds circling. They glide above you, each seeming as light as air. You imagine what it feels like to be one of them. Flying gives you the feeling of freedom, without a care in the world. What wonderful things can you see below you? Just let the breeze carry you, around and around in gentle circles. The air is warm and fresh. You can hover here as long as you like. When you are ready, return your focus to the beach, with all its wonderful sights and smells. Breathing deeply, all you hear is the sound of the sea.

My heavenly guide
is always by my side.

ANGEL DREAMS

You are resting on the softest bed you have ever felt, relaxed and comfortable. Looking up, you see the twilight sky, and discover you're lying on a cloud. You feel warm and secure. Taking a few slow, deep breaths, your body begins to feel heavy, and sinks into the cloud. Draw each breath deep inside you. Feel your breath reach every part of your body as you inhale. Let your stomach fall easily as you exhale.

The sky changes in colour from a soft pink at the horizon, to a cobalt blue above. Faintly, you see a few stars beginning to come out. You breathe in and out slowly, taking in the beauty of the sky. Your mind is calm, and you feel very peaceful. A twinkle in the distance grows larger as it comes closer to you. Drawing nearer, you see it is an angel. She is surrounded by a soft white light. Her delicate gown glistens and sparkles as she moves. As she hovers above you, you are bathed in the light. She smiles at you and seems to speak without talking. You are filled with love and happiness. It is a warm feeling that spreads from your head to your toes. You breathe in and out slowly, and your body feels very relaxed. Your angel remains beside you as you rest, and you feel very loved. Gently stretch, remembering where you are laying, before you get up.

My imagination takes me
to wonderful places.

FAIRY GARDEN

Your bed feels soft and warm, and you seem to sink into the fluffy mattress. It feels like laying in cotton wool. Sleepily, you take long, deep breaths. You are relaxed and peaceful. Looking around, you see that you are resting in a matchbox on dandelion down. Beside you stands the prettiest fairy you have ever seen. She smiles at you and holds out her hand. Her shiny wings glitter and sparkle as the light catches them. You feel happy, and reach out to take her hand.

Magically, while holding her hand, you are able to fly too. As you breathe slowly in and out, your body becomes as light as air. The feeling reaches every part of your body, right down to the ends of your toes. The fairy holds your hand securely, and starts to flutter her wings. Slowly you rise, as she gently guides you. You float easily, continuing to breathe slowly.

Below you now, you see a beautiful garden. There are flowers of every shape and colour. Their perfume delights your nose as you breathe in. Take some time to look around the garden. It is filled with your favourite flowers. Tall, shady trees invite you to sit beneath them. This is the perfect spot to daydream, or think of nothing at all. The fairy tells you that this is your own special garden, and you may visit whenever you wish. She smiles as she guides you back. You happily return to the matchbox to rest. The fairy leans down and kisses you lightly on the cheek. It tingles magically. You relax and remember the beauty of your garden. You are peaceful and relaxed in your fairy bed.

With strength and courage
I can achieve great things.

COURAGE

You are lying in the sun, on soft dry grass. Your body feels warm and relaxed. Slowly you stretch out, and you are very comfortable. You are a great lion, king of beasts. A gentle breeze stirs the grass, and birds chirp happily in the trees. As you breathe slowly and deeply, you feel your strength grow. It fills your body, all the way down your arms and legs. You feel powerful, and you have great courage.

A grasshopper lands close to you. Watching as it hops around in the undergrowth, you realize that it has a mighty leap for such a tiny creature. You are also capable of great things. Imagine yourself in a situation that is difficult for you. What things could you do to make it better? Now see yourself doing those things. Picture the happy ending that you create. The things that make you feel afraid can be overcome. Believe in yourself, and you can do anything. You are strong and courageous. See yourself doing something that you were afraid of doing before. Breathe deeply, remembering how it feels to be determined and confident. Knowing that you may always call upon this inner strength, store it somewhere deep inside you. Gently stretch your powerful arms and legs, and return to your surroundings.

Although gone from this world,
you live in my heart forever.

GOODBYE

Settle yourself comfortably, and concentrate on breathing slowly and deeply. A warm feeling of relaxation spreads from your toes to the top of your head. Your body feels heavy and seems to sink towards the ground. As you breathe slowly, you are calm and secure. Each time you inhale, your breath goes deeper inside you. Hold it for just a moment, then gently exhale.

You may feel a mixture of strange emotions, and some may be new to you. You may not really know how you feel, but that's okay. Know that you are loved very much by the people around you, as well as the person you've had to say goodbye to. Saying goodbye to someone you love is very hard. Remember a special time that you shared together. What was it that made that time so special? You also remember their smiling face, and the love you feel coming from them.

Imagine this love is a bright white light that fills your body. As you breathe in and out, the rich stream of energising light pours in through your head, and out the ends of your fingers and toes. You feel full of strength and love. You have been given the gift of memories and happiness from this person, and you may carry this love with you always. Rest now, your body is light and your mind is peaceful. When you are ready, become aware again of your surroundings. Take a few moments before you decide to get up.

Nature's colours balance
and heal my body.

RAINBOW

Close your eyes and picture yourself on a green hillside. A gentle breeze stirs the soft grass that you rest on. The sun fights to beam down its rays through the fluffy clouds. A few drops of rain fall gently around you, but you are warm and dry. The smell of spring fills your nose as you take long, deep breaths. You feel calm and peaceful.

Something wondrous begins to appear in the sky. A rainbow unfolds like a giant slippery slide, stretching all the way to the ground. Its radiant colours seem to challenge the sun in splendour. You see that the rainbow lands right where you are. Little by little, its colours begin to wash over you.

The colour red starts at your toes and gradually moves up your legs. They feel relaxed and heavy. Focus on the colour red. What things can you picture that are red? An apple, or a clown's nose perhaps. As the colour spreads, so does the feeling of relaxation.

Towards your stomach, it turns orange. Breathe deeply, thinking of objects that are orange. Fruit can be orange, or even a traffic light. Think of your favourite things that are orange. Your stomach now is changing to yellow, like a daffodil, or the sun. Yellow has energy and lifts your spirits. Feel this energy fill you as you breathe in. Reaching your chest now, the colour becomes green, Mother Nature's favourite. Think of all the different shades of green we see in plants and trees. Imagine your favourite place that has lots of trees and plants. Maybe it is a park, or a forest, or your own garden. The flow of colour continues up your body and at your neck, it becomes blue. What are your favourite blue things? An azure sky, or maybe the shimmering ocean? Blue changes to purple as the rainbow moves up to your head. Centre your thoughts on things that are purple. Many flowers are this colour, like violets and lavender. Breathe slowly, drawing the colour into your body as you inhale. Your body now is completely relaxed and calm. If there are any parts of your body that ache or feel pain, imagine the rainbow flowing to that place. It cleanses away any lingering hurt, leaving you completely relaxed. Take a few moments to enjoy how free and harmonious your body feels. When you are ready, awaken to your surroundings, and gently stretch.

I am strong, competent,
and have special abilities.

SUPER HERO

Settle yourself into a comfortable position, and take a few moments to relax your body. Scrunch up your toes tightly, and then let them go. Feel the muscles in your legs loosen, as the sensation spreads up your body. Clench your fists, then let your hands fall open, as you consciously relax your arms. Your body seems to sink towards the ground. Take long slow breaths, filling your lungs, and slowly exhale. Feel any tension or aches drain away. Imagine you are expelling them out your mouth as you exhale.

Some super heroes have special powers like that. Maybe you have special powers too? Imagine that your breath can blow clouds in the sky. What other powers would you like to have? You might want to be the strongest person in the world. Fill your body with strength as you breathe in. Each time you breathe, you grow stronger. Your body is powerful and invincible.

If you have any areas of your body that don't feel strong, imagine waves of special strength flowing to that spot. What other super powers would you like to have? You may like to fly, and you can if you want to. Picture yourself ready for flight. Behind you, your cape flaps in the breeze. What colour costume would you wear? As you breathe in and out, your body becomes lighter. You feel calm and secure.

When you are ready, prepare for take off. See yourself stretching your arms up, and lifting off the ground. You fly effortlessly, and can go as fast or as slow as you wish. What wonderful things do you see below you? Perhaps you see buildings and people, or a beautiful landscape. You may even visit places that you have never been to before. Take your time to look around, you are in control.

When you are ready, return to your home, and gently land where you started. Focus on where you are resting. How did it feel to fly? Remember the feeling of strength filling your body as you breathe with slow, even breaths. You can do this any time you wish, because you are a super hero.

The tranquility of nature
refreshes and cleanses my soul.

WATERFALL

You find yourself in a beautiful rainforest. All around are lush, green plants. Some colourful, exotic flowers bloom; their perfume hangs in the air. Breathe in deeply the smell of the rainforest. Let it fill your lungs each time you inhale, and gently exhale.

The sound of rushing water beckons you. A waterfall tumbles down from rocky outcrops. The water looks so inviting, you decide to try it. It is cool and refreshing, as it gently flows over your body. A symphony of nature, it tinkles and trickles, as it falls around you. You feel calm and happy.

As the water cascades over you, your body begins to relax. The sensation spreads from your head, all the way to your toes. Feel it relaxing your head and shoulders, then gradually down through your body to your legs. Like a shower, it washes away any aches or pains. Your body is as free and as fluid as the water around you. Breathe slowly and deeply, focusing on how tranquil you feel. For a moment, clear your mind to simply enjoy the harmony of your surroundings. Use your waterfall any time you want to cleanse away worries or pain. Here in your waterfall there is nothing but peace and serenity. Take these feelings with you, as you return slowly to the physical world.

I feel a part of nature and connected to other creatures.

DOLPHIN

Close your eyes and imagine an undersea world. The sunlight casts playful shadows that dance in the water around you. Marvellous creatures of all shapes and sizes go about their business. Like a prism, the water seems to intensify their bright colours. Concentrate on breathing slowly, filling your lungs each time, and gently exhaling. Don't strain or force your breath, just let your chest rise and fall comfortably. No need to worry, you are able to breathe easily underwater.

Now feel yourself relax, as if you were floating effortlessly. The water frees your body, but also supports you. Instead of arms and legs, imagine that you have flippers and a tail. Gliding smoothly, you move through the water. All you feel is the water caressing your smooth skin. There are other dolphins around you now. They frolic and play together happily. Tumble and roll with them in their playful games. Somehow that cheeky sparkle in their eyes seems to lift your spirits, and you feel a wonderful connection with them. Maintain your breathing evenly, as it fills your body with lightness and calm. Spend time lingering with your dolphin friends if you wish. Explore their ocean world, which is quiet and serene, yet full of life.

You feel a magical energy flowing everywhere, and it feels a part of you. It feels wonderful to be absorbed by the beauty around you. When you are ready, your dolphin friends will guide you back home.

I have the courage to challenge myself and discover new things.

OUTER SPACE

Close your eyes, and in your mind you are going to a special place. It's time to prepare for your journey into outer space. You are settled comfortably in your space ship, and begin to take slow, even breaths. Feel your stomach expand as you inhale, then let it fall as you gently exhale. Continue to focus on your breathing, as you take in your surroundings.

Millions of stars twinkle against the black velvet void. Like lingering fireworks, swirling gases of every colour illuminate the sky. Your body begins to relax as you steadily draw in and out your breath. Beginning at your toes, a feeling of heaviness creeps up your legs. It spreads through your body, your arms and your head. Gravity holds you as though you were made of lead. Turn your head a little to see the moon out your window. You must be closer to it than anyone else in the universe. It seems to shine it's incandescent light just for you. Imagine that light flowing into your body through the top of your head. The light particles travel in your veins to every part of your body. As you breathe in, the energising light fills you and flows out the ends of your fingers and toes. Your body feels light and radiates warmth.

Like an astronaut you are weightless in your space

ship. Here you are free, free from pain or any worries you may have. In the distance, a tiny star whizzes across the sky in front of you. Why not make a wish? Would you wish for a special gift for yourself, or someone else? Maybe you wished to change a situation that is difficult, or doesn't seem fair. Wishes do come true, but not always in the way we want them to. Answers can take a while, and sometimes we have to look really hard to find the gift.

Picture your wish coming true, and how it makes you feel. Happiness and joy fill you like the moon's rays as you breathe in and out. You feel peace and contentment as you look upon the vast skies. The universe makes no judgements of you. All it expects is that you be the best person you can, and treat other beings with respect. When your journey is complete, your space craft is ready to return home. Remember to focus on your surroundings, and gently stretch before you leave your spaceship.

Every experience
helps me to grow.

SEED OF TRUTH

Now it is time for you to rest and relax. Time for you to focus on yourself, and nobody else. Begin with a deep breath, and as you breathe in, let your stomach expand. As you exhale, let your stomach fall gently. Continue to take deep regular breaths. Imagine it being drawn deep into your body. Let this sensation fill every part of you. With each breath, you are more and more relaxed. Your body starts to feel heavy, as if it is being pulled toward the floor by a magnet.

Take a few moments now to appreciate how comfortable and peaceful you feel. This is your own special time. Use it to think about your dreams and wishes. Picture them coming true. What a wonderful feeling. You are a unique and valuable person, capable of achieving great things. Accept that you are different from other people, as we all are. These are the things that make us special. Everyone makes mistakes too, but it is important that you learn from them. You can overcome things that frighten you by drawing on your own ability and inner strength. Experience helps us to grow and learn. Every creature starts out small and vulnerable. Look for the truth, and know that you are connected to everyone and everything. Return your focus to your body now. Continue your slow, even breathing, and feel yourself filled with energy. Become aware of your surroundings and wriggle your toes. Calm and confident, know that you are loved by people around you, and that your life has purpose.

I can sleep
safely and peacefully.

SWEET DREAMS

How wonderful to be settled comfortably in your own bed, ready to go to sleep. The bed feels so cosy. You are warm and snug. Here you are safe, your bed is safe and your room is safe. You are protected from the world. Take a long, slow breath, drawing it in as far as you can without forcing. Now gently breathe out, letting your stomach fall easily. Continue breathing like this; each breath fills you all the way down to your toes.

Relaxed, and feeling heavy, your body seems to sink into the bed. Perhaps you have trouble falling asleep, or sometimes dreams may bother you? Worries are a normal part of life, and you can learn to deal with them in a good way. You are powerful, and capable of changing things. Use your imagination to conquer the monsters in your dreams.

What things could you do to confront them? In your mind, see yourself defeating them. There are many ways you can win. You are in control. Now that you have overcome these worries, imagine that they are birds and let them disappear up into the sky. You feel strong and confident. Take a few moments to enjoy the feeling. Return your attention to your breathing. Continue taking deep, even breaths. Your body is light and free, and without a care in the world. If any worries return to try to bother you, release them up into the sky again. Know that you have the strength and courage to deal with them. Remember, you are safe and protected in your bed. Bring your attention back to the room you are in. It feels familiar and secure. You can sleep happily and comfortably. It's easy now that you know how.

I will always be loved,
even by those who are gone.

LOVE FROM ABOVE

Settle yourself in a comfortable spot. Gently stretch and wriggle a little until you feel just right. Take in a long, slow breath, filling your lungs, then gently exhale. Let your stomach rise and fall easily. Imagine your breath going deep inside you. It travels to every part of your body.

You begin to feel very relaxed. A warm sensation spreads from your toes, and gradually travels up your body. Clench the muscles in your legs tightly for a few seconds, then release them. Feel any tension released from your back and stomach muscles. Make a tight fist with your hands, and then release. Your body is completely relaxed. It feels heavy, and is drawn towards the floor. Continue taking slow, even breaths.

Your body is free of any discomfort. Perhaps there is pain though in your heart and mind. It's OK to feel hurt when you have lost someone you love. You may feel scared to be without them. Letting go of the pain you feel does not mean you are letting go of them. Think of something special that you shared with this person. You will always have a special connection to them. It's all right to feel happy when you think of them. Realize that they are not gone from your world, but now part of them is in everything. They will always be a part of the things that you shared together. Many things may change, but some will not. You will always be loved, and can continue to love them.

As you inhale, imagine their love is a shimmering white light that fills you. With each breath, it grows brighter and more intense. This energising light is full of strength and love. It flows everywhere, connecting everything. Know that you will always have that connection within you. Bring your attention back to your surroundings. You feel peaceful and refreshed. Take a few moments to stretch and wriggle again before opening your eyes.

I love and value myself,
and treat others with respect.

BE TRUE TO YOU

Settle yourself into a position that is comfortable. Now, starting at your toes, imagine a lovely warm feeling of relaxation is spreading slowly up your body. Your feet and legs feel floppy and a little heavy. The sensation moves up through your body, relaxing your stomach and chest. Shrug your shoulders, then release them. The feeling travels down your arms to your fingers. Let your hands rest, open and relaxed.

Take in a deep breath, hold it for just a second, then gently release it. Repeat this a few times. Try to keep a slow, even rhythm to your breathing. As you breathe in, your stomach expands, then gently falls as you exhale. Each time you inhale, imagine that you are drawing in strength and courage. It fills your lungs and expands through your body.

You are a special and unique person. Sometimes other people do and say things that may hurt or frighten you. Maybe they say that you are too short or too fat, or different in some way? The truth is that their hurtful actions really have nothing to do with you. It comes from their own feelings about themselves. Some people try to make themselves seem bigger or more powerful by making others feel small.

No one can take your power away from you unless you let them. Show that you are courageous and strong by not believing what they say. Picture yourself standing up to them, and be proud. Try to forgive them, as it takes away their power over you. You don't have to be who they say you are. Know yourself and accept that your differences are what makes you special.

Treat others with respect, and kindness will be returned to you. Know that you have the love and support of your family and friends. Take a deep breath, and feel yourself filled with love and confidence. Remember this feeling and carry it in your heart. When you are ready, bring your attention back to the room you are in. Wriggle your fingers and toes and stretch gently before getting up.

I draw upon the universe,
and seek its healing energies.

HEALING LIGHT

Find yourself a comfortable place to lay. Your arms rest by your sides and your hands fall open naturally. Let your feet relax and fall into their own position. Imagine that your body is growing heavy, and seems to sink towards the floor. It feels like you are being drawn by a magnet.

A wonderful sensation of relaxation spreads throughout your body. It travels all the way from your toes to the top of your head. Your arms and legs feel too heavy to lift. Focus now on your breathing. Take in a long, slow breath through your nose. Your chest and stomach expand as you breathe in. Hold it for just a moment, then gently exhale.

Repeat this a few times until your breathing becomes slow and regular. Don't try to force your breathing, just let your lungs do the work. Imagine that they are a giant set of bellows that draw the air in as they expand, and release it as they slowly close. Feel your breath going deep into your body as you inhale. It fills you with peace and harmony. You are completely relaxed.

Now as you breathe in, picture a bright white light fill you and travel throughout your body. It shimmers and radiates all the way to the ends of your fingers and toes. Each time you inhale, the rich stream of light grows brighter.

You feel your whole body pulsating with energy. Focus now on any areas of sickness or pain that you may have. With your mind, direct the healing light to that area. Imagine that the tiny cells in your body are little soldiers, fighting to heal you. They battle endlessly, never giving up. Picture them victorious, as they soothe away illness and pain. As you breathe out, the enemy is expelled out your mouth. Feel the energising light replenish and refresh you as it flows through your body. Focus on this area as long as you wish, continuing to send light to your little soldiers in their battle. You are full of strength and love. Enjoy how your body feels, and rest in this position for a while. When you are ready, return your thoughts to the room you are in. Take a few moments to remember where you are. Gently stretch and wriggle your fingers and toes.

I grow, I experience, I learn.

THE TREE

The sun beams cheerily on you, as you find an inviting place to rest and lie down. Looking up, you see some magnificent trees towering above you. Imagine what it would be like to be one of them. Stretch your arms and legs out straight, arms beside you, like a giant tree trunk. Don't hold them stiffly, but let them now relax into place. Pretend that you have roots growing out the bottom of your feet that anchor you into the ground. Like a tree, you can draw in magical, life-giving energy from the earth.

As you draw this energy from the ground, it travels up your legs, through your body and down your arms. It pulsates your body, spreading a wonderful feeling of relaxation. Your whole body feels like it's weighed down; your arms and legs are too heavy to lift. Take long, slow breaths as you focus on relaxing every tiny part of your body. With each breath you become more and more relaxed.

Imagine your breath going deep inside your body. It travels through you like sap inside the tree's veins. Every part of your body is nourished. You are filled with a bright, glowing energy.

Sunlight warms the top of your head, as it does the

fluttering leaves. Draw it into your body from above. A stream of golden light fills you, and you feel energised and refreshed. This light helps you to grow, just as the sun makes the trees and plants grow. It flows everywhere, connecting everything. Even the birds in the trees need this energy.

Look around you to enjoy the wonderful things that nature creates. From a tangerine sunset to a bumble bee's buzz, there is beauty in everything. You feel peaceful and happy as you appreciate the harmony of the world around you. When you are ready, flutter your fingers and toes. Stretch any stiffness from your tree trunk. Remind yourself where you have rested, and focus again on your surroundings.

I place no limits
on what I can achieve.

BALLOON RIDE

Choose yourself a comfortable position, because today you are going to take a special journey. Breathe in a long slow breath, holding it for just a moment, then release it gently, letting the air escape without forcing. Fill your lungs deeply, as if you were filling a balloon. Imagine you can smell the sweet morning air as it fills your nose. It is the delightful smell of the countryside.

Now it is time to board your balloon basket. What colour is your balloon? It can be any colour or design that you wish. See the bright colours highlighted against the blue sky. As your balloon lifts slowly, you feel safe and secure. You are in control, and your balloon will take you anywhere you wish. The earth below is a myriad of shades of green, brown, and blue. The fresh breeze fills your nostrils, and smells like freedom. As you soar between heaven and earth, there are no limits. Problems seem much smaller up here. How would your life be different if there were no limits put upon you? What things would you do? See yourself doing one of those things; you do it well. Maybe it is creative, or just for fun. Take a few moments to enjoy the freedom and peace that you have. Breathe slowly and evenly, your body totally relaxed.

Look below you now, a river winds it's way through

the countryside. You remember seeing it before, and you know that if you follow the river, it will always lead you home. When you feel ready, your balloon will gently land for you to alight. Climb out and feel the earth beneath your feet. Your balloon stays tethered, ready to fly another day.

My two families make me
even more special.

MERMAID TALE

The sun warms your body as you rest peacefully. The aroma of salty air fills your nose as you breathe slowly and evenly. You are sunning yourself beside the sea. Looking down, you see that you have a fish's tail instead of legs. Stretch your legs out, imagining that you have a powerful, graceful tail. Perhaps you would like to take a swim, the water looks so inviting. Don't worry, you can breathe easily underwater. You swim and dive; the water feeling cool and refreshing against your skin. What wonderful creatures do you see? The other fish seem to smile at you. You are not just a fish, and not just human. A mermaid has two families, just like some of us do. Sometimes you might feel like you don't really belong to either, but a mermaid is even more special because it is different. What things are special about your two families? Perhaps you have new brothers or sisters. New families bring new opportunities for love and friendship. How lucky you are to have so many people that love you. Spend time playing with your underwater family. You feel happy and relaxed. Remember that wonderful feeling of belonging to something special. Your fishy friends will guide you home, and are always there for your return.

I see magic
in the most ordinary things.

A UNIQUE HORN

Rest your head, sweet child, and be delighted by tales of a special creature. Your body begins to relax as you breathe slowly and consistently. Focus on any areas that feel uncomfortable. Draw your breath deep into your body, and imagine it going to that spot. You are now completely relaxed.

A magical creature, the unicorn, was the last horse to have a horn. He often felt alone. When he saw the other horses, he wanted nothing more than to belong. He knew that he was not like them. Imagine that you are the unicorn. What things do you think are different about you? What the unicorn didn't realize is that he is more special because he is different. To his surprise, it wasn't only his horn that was unusual. Unicorns have special gifts that can't be seen with your eyes. They are sensitive animals that can see truth and beauty with their hearts. They are also free spirited and wise, showing strength and courage. They accept differences in others without judgement. To the unicorn though, all he could see was that he must be ugly because of his horn. There was nothing he could do about it, so he just decided to be himself. The other horses began to see with their hearts, not their eyes, and realized that the unicorn was something extra special. So the unicorn lived happily with the other horses, teaching them compassion, forgiveness and to seek their own differences. Unicorns are very valuable animals, so these days they keep their horns hidden. They do not look different, but are special inside. Are you a unicorn, and would you recognise one if you saw it? Bring your attention back now to where you rest. You feel refreshed and peaceful. When you are ready, wriggle your fingers and toes awhile before getting up.

I drift, relaxed and peaceful.

RIVER DRIFT

Climb aboard the little boat and find yourself a cosy place to rest. Picture in your mind a small winding stream with fresh, clear water. All around are lush green trees and plants. It is a beautiful sunny day. You feel happy and secure stretched out on pillows and cushions. Draw in a long slow breath to enjoy the delightful scents of nature. Allow your breath to go deep into your lungs, expanding your stomach, then gently release. Continue breathing like this.

Trees that overhang the river cast leafy shadows as you drift past. You begin to relax. Feel a heaviness that starts at your feet, and begins to travel up your legs. Allow this sensation to spread through your body and into your arms, right to the tips of your fingers. Breathe slowly and evenly, allowing every part of your body to feel relaxed. Your boat guides itself as it glides over the sparkling water. The sound of the water lapping at the boat lulls you as it meanders down stream. You have nothing to think about but drifting and enjoying the beauty of nature. Birds that you pass chirp 'hello', while insects busily hum in the long grasses. You float past a vivid green frog, watching you from the river bank. Relaxed, your body feels light and free. Imagine drawing in sunlight through the top of your head. It fills you with wonderful pulsating energy. Allow it to go deeper inside you as you inhale. Drift happily, filled with light and love, for as long as you wish. When you are ready to return, just around the next bend of the river, you will find you are back where you began. Stretch out your arms and wriggle a little, before getting up.

I draw upon the earth's energy
and feel connected to nature.

MOUNTAIN VIEW

Today as you rest, you find yourself on a mountain top. Close your eyes to see wonderful things. The sky is clear, and you can see forever. Create a beautiful scene in your mind. Perhaps you see forests and hills, or even the ocean in the distance. Allow yourself to breathe slowly and easily, focusing on drawing your breath deep inside your body. Here you are safe and comfortable. You sense a special connection to the earth, like an energy drawn up from the ground through your feet. It fills you, spreading relaxation and calm. You feel very much a part of the world, sharing this place with plants and animals around you. Energy flows everywhere, connecting everything. The sun beams down, warming you with its golden rays. Imagine this stream of light pouring in through the top of your head. It is a beautiful energising light, filled with strength and love. Your heart and mind feel free. Focus on your breathing, drawing the light deep inside you, and out the ends of your toes and fingers. Remember how you are feeling, as you can draw this energy from nature whenever you wish. Stretch gently and take a few moments before you rise.

With the courage to be myself,
I am beautiful.

THE UGLY BUTTERFLY

Find yourself a spot that's cosy, stretch out fully, and relax. Calm your body and focus your mind by breathing deeply and evenly. Let go of any worries that you might have. Give them wings, and see them fly off into the distance. Think only about relaxing your body and breathing slowly. Your body feels heavy now, like it's sinking into the floor. In your mind now, imagine a little caterpillar, grey and hairy. At first he's not very attractive. Caterpillars are a lot like us, they change as they grow, just like we do. The caterpillar doesn't know what he will look like, or what he will become. He just knows instinctively what to do. Weaving his silk cocoon is a huge task for him, and requires much inner strength. The butterfly struggles to emerge as his true self. His magnificent, brightly coloured wings are a sight to behold. Nature creates beauty in many ways. It's OK to like yourself, and wonderful to just be yourself. Love your body, and the things it can do, even if it's different to everyone else. Picture yourself with butterfly wings. What colour would yours be? Remember, the courage to be yourself, is beautiful to others.

Focus again on your breathing, and slowly bring your attention back to the room you are in. Stretch gently before getting up.

I have imagination and I am creative.

CLOUDS

Close your eyes to rest and relax. A brightly coloured rug is where you lay, stretched out on the soft green grass. You are warm and comfortable. Become aware of your breathing, and take gentle, slow breaths. Draw the air in through your nose, hold for a moment, then release it slowly. Move through each part of your body with your mind, focusing on any areas that feel uncomfortable or tense. Let your breath go deep inside your stomach. You feel more relaxed with each breath.

Visualize your surroundings now. Look up at the never-ending blue sky. Fluffy clouds drift silently across in front of you. Pictures appear and change before your eyes, as wispy fragments move with the breeze. Let your mind soar with the clouds. What pictures do you see? Perhaps you see animals, plants, or magical creatures. Take a few moments to relax and watch the images float by. Your imagination is as vast as the endless sky. It is continually changing, bringing new images and creative ideas. Imagine you are breathing in sunshine as you draw the air deep inside your body. Experience the wonderful energy of nature and the feeling of happiness that it brings. Think positive and appreciate all the wonderful things in your life. You are a very special part of this world, and have something valuable to contribute.

When you are ready, return your focus to your surroundings. Gently stretch out your legs and arms. You feel happy and energised.

I can protect my feelings
to be safe and happy.

PROTECTION

Position yourself comfortably, and begin to think about your breathing. Draw your breath deep inside you, expanding your stomach. Gently breathe out, creating a slow rhythm.

Imagine that invisible roots grow from the bottom of your feet into the ground. Connect with the earth's energy, making you feel sturdy and balanced. Centre yourself by finding that quiet place deep inside you. It is that space between breathing in, and letting your breath out. It is silent, peaceful and comfortable. Breathe deeply, sensing this place, knowing that you have your own special power within. This calm and timeless spirit gives you guidance when you feel no one else can help you.

Sometimes energy from other people can make you feel bad or sick, even without them actually doing any-thing. You can protect yourself from other people's unhappy feelings. Picture yourself surrounded by a bubble, shiny and bright, big enough just for you. This bubble makes you safe, only allowing happy, positive things to pass through it. Whenever you feel hurt or threatened, create the bubble around you. You will feel cheery and filled with bright light. Take some time to look inside to your spirit, to feel safe and confident again. Think about slow, deep breathing. Remember, this is your own special tool, to use whenever you need it.

I am capable of
making good choices.

TREE HOUSE

Find yourself a comfortable place to rest. Focus on how your body is feeling as you begin to relax. Are any parts feeling tired or sore? Concentrate on softening those places. Breathe slowly and deeply, letting your stomach rise and fall easily.

Today we will journey to a special place, somewhere that's just for you. Imagine that you are walking on lush green grass. There are trees around you that sway gently in the soft breeze. Hear their leaves rustle with the sound of birds chirping in the tree tops. The sun shines brightly, making you feel warm and happy. What other things do you notice around you? Perhaps you notice the sweet smell of flowers nearby.

Not far away you see a really tall tree. It has a huge trunk and thick woody branches. Walk closer to the tree, and see every detail. It's sturdy branches grow near to the ground. Why don't you climb it? The branches are strong and grow close together, so it's easy to go up. About halfway up you see a great spot to rest. It is a tree house. You decide to climb inside, and find it's very comfortable. You have a great view from up here. What things can you see?

This is a special place, a place you can come to think, to

rest or to solve problems. It is peaceful and safe, and you can stay as long as you like. In your mind, pretend to see the problem you are having. What choices can you make? What things could you do to try and solve it? Picture what happens, and see yourself successful. You are capable of making good choices, and creating great things. Think about how you feel when you have done something terrific. You are happy and confident. Light and energy fills you as your spirits soar. Breathe deeply, drawing in this wonderful feeling with each breath. Let your body remember this feeling too. When you are refreshed and ready, you can climb down from your tree house and return home. Come back whenever you wish, it is your place.

I try to do good things
and see the good in others.

ASPIRATION

Lie down on your back, with your arms by your side, and your legs straight. Gently stretch them as far as you can, hold it for a moment, then relax. Let your body become loose and floppy. Feel it sink towards the floor. Close your eyes and breathe slowly.

Now, picture that you have a beautiful sunbeam shining down on you. The bright, golden light makes you warm and peaceful. As you breathe in, pretend that the light goes deep inside your body. It fills every tiny part of you, making you feel tingly and alive.

Imagine the light going through the top of your head. It energises and transforms you. Your eyes will see only the beauty in things. Your nose will smell only sweet essences, and enjoy the purity of clean, fresh air. Your mouth will savour the goodness of Mother Nature's food. It will speak only the truth, and with respect. Your ears will hear the sound of our living earth and its creatures.

The light continues to spread through your body. Your arms feel strong, for lifting, playing and creating. Your legs too, for running and leaping from one obstacle to the next with hope and enthusiasm. Your heart beats boldly, filled with a generous love and accepts differences without judgement. You feel wonderful all over. Draw your breath in and out slowly. Rest and think about how you feel. In a few moments, stretch gently and open your eyes.